D0470818

MAY 1 1

EXTREME NATURE

DESERT EXTREMES

NATALIE HYDE

Crabtree Publishing Company
www.crabtreebooks.com

Crabtree Publishing Company

www.crabtreebooks.com

Author: Natalie Hyde

Editor: Molly Aloian

Proofreaders: Adrianna Morganelli,
Crystal Sikkens, Katherine Berti

Project coordinator: Robert Walker

Production coordinator: Margaret Amy Salter

Prepress technician: Margaret Amy Salter

Project editor: Tom Jackson

Designer: Lynne Lennon

Picture researchers: Sophie Mortimer, Sean Hannaway

Managing editor: Tim Harris

Art director: Jeni Child

Design manager: David Poole

Editorial director: Lindsey Lowe

Children's publisher: Anne O'Daly

Photographs:
Corbis: Chris Mattison: page 15; Michael & Patricia Fogden:
pages 16 (right), 21 (bottom); Rod Patterson: page 19 (top);
Wolfgang Kaehler: pages 22-23; John Carnemolla:
page 24 (center right); Ryan Pyle: page 29 (top)
Photoshot: Martin Harvey: page 14; Daniel Heuclin:
pages 17 (bottom), 20-21
Photos.com: front cover
Shutterstock: Galyna Andrushko: pages 4-5;
Angel's Gate Photography: page 5 (top); Doug Lemke:
page 5 (bottom); Donal Mullins: page 6; Amp: pages 6-7;
Mike Norton: pages 7, 12; Dimitry Pichugin: pages 8-9;
Christa DeRidder: page 8; Dr. Morley Read: page 9;
Ekaterina Vysokova: page 10; Indigo Fish: pages 10-11;
Katrina Leigh: page 11 (top); Muriel Lasure: page 11 (bottom);
EcoPrint: page 13 (top); Judy Crawford: page 13 (bottom);
Johan Swanepoel: pages 14-15; Kristian Sekulic: page 16 (left);
Hagit Berkovich: page 17 (top); Colin & Linda McKie: page 18;
Steve Lovegrove: pages 18-19; Rusty Dodson: page 19 (bottom);
Roman Kolbabek: page 20 (top); Andrey Petrov: page 21 (top);
Daniel Gilbey: page 22 (bottom); Jarno Gonzalez Zarraonandia:
page 23 (center right); Vera Bogaerts: pages 23 (bottom left),
27 (bottom); John S. Sfondilias: pages 24-25; Weldon Schloneger:
page 25 (top); Sebastian Selzer: page 26; Michael Ledray:
page 27 (top); Alessio Ponti: page 27 (center); Amee Cross:
page 28 (top); Bruno Ismael Da Silva Alves: page 28 (bottom);
Ronald Sumners: page 29 (bottom)

Every effort has been made to trace the owners of
copyrighted material.

Library and Archives Canada Cataloguing in Publication

Hyde, Natalie, 1963-
Desert extremes / Natalie Hyde.

(Extreme nature)
Includes index.
ISBN 978-0-7787-4500-6 (bound).--ISBN 978-0-7787-4517-4 (pbk.)

1. Desert ecology--Juvenile literature. 2. Desert animals--Juvenile
literature. 3. Desert plants--Juvenile literature. 4. Deserts--Juvenile
literature. I. Title. II. Series: Extreme nature (St. Catharines, Ont.)

QH541.5.D4H93 2008   j577.54   C2008-907342-8

Library of Congress Cataloging-in-Publication Data

Hyde, Natalie, 1963-
Desert extremes / Natalie Hyde.
p. cm. -- (Extreme nature)
Includes index.
ISBN 978-0-7787-4517-4 (pbk. : alk. paper) -- ISBN 978-0-7787-4500-6
(reinforced library binding : alk. paper)
1. Deserts--Juvenile literature. 2. Desert ecology--Juvenile literature. I.
Title. II. Series.

QH541.5.D4H94 2008
578.754--dc22

2008048638

Crabtree Publishing Company

www.crabtreebooks.com   1-800-387-7650

Published in Canada
Crabtree Publishing
616 Welland Ave.
St. Catharines, Ontario
L2M 5V6

Published in the United States
Crabtree Publishing
PMB16A
350 Fifth Ave., Suite 3308
New York, NY 10118

CONTENTS

INTRODUCTION

Deserts are places that receive less than 10 inches (25 cm) of rain each year. The areas around the North Pole and South Pole could be called cold deserts because there is no rain or liquid water of any kind—it is all frozen solid. However, most deserts are very hot and lie in a warm part of the world called the **tropics**.

THE WORLD'S DESERTS

The Sahara is the largest desert in the world. It stretches across northern Africa and is about the size of the United States. The Kalahari in southern Africa is known for its huge red sand dunes. The color comes from iron **minerals**. In some places, the sand is 200 feet (60 m) deep. The Arabian Desert has the world's largest area of sand. The Rub'al-Khali, which means "Empty Quarter," is an area in Arabia the size of Texas that is completely covered in dunes.

▶ Deserts are sometimes described as "seas of sand." The best way of crossing the sand sea is on a "ship of the desert." This is the nickname for camels—large hoofed animals that have been used by desert people for thousands of years.

MAKING DESERTS

Some deserts form where mountains block moist ocean air. Areas far from the oceans have dry winds that soak up any moisture. However, some deserts form beside the ocean! Cool water currents chill the air and this draws dry wind off the land, rather than blowing moist wind onto it.

DESERT LANDS

The Gobi Desert in northern China and Mongolia does not have much sand at all—it is mostly bare rock. *Gobi* means "waterless place." Australia is also very dry—it is the driest **continent** on Earth. One-third of Australia is dry enough to be desert.

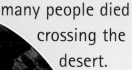

In the Extreme

Death Valley is in the Mojave Desert of California. It is the lowest point in North America and also the hottest—it reaches 134 °F (57 °C) in summer. Death Valley was named during a **gold rush** in 1849 because many people died crossing the desert.

COMPLETELY DRY

The driest place on Earth is the Atacama Desert in Chile, South America. It has had the world's longest **drought**. No rain fell for 420 years—the first shower arrived in 1991. It is so dry that no life has been found in the soil. This has been helpful for **NASA**. They used the desert to test instruments for missions to the planet Mars.

GOING HOT AND COLD

It is always dry in a desert but it does not stay hot all the time. During the day, the clear sky allows the Sun's heat to scorch the surface. At night, a cloudless sky works in the opposite way. Clouds keep heat near to the ground, but clear desert skies allow the heat to escape. It gets cold after sunset. During the day, temperatures are often more than 100 °F (37 °C). However, at night the temperature can drop to 32 °F (0 °C).

▲ Some riverbeds in the Atacama Desert have been dry for 120,000 years. They have been covered in cracked mud.

▲ Nearly all of the rain that falls on the south side of Arizona's Grand Canyon flows into one creek. This creek forms the Havasu Falls, making an area of green within the dry canyon.

SALTY SEAS

There are a few areas of water in deserts. For example, the Dead Sea in the Middle East is formed by the Jordan River. The river does not flow to the ocean but into a deep **basin** in the desert. The water **evaporates**, and as the water turns to **vapor**, the salt in it stays in the water left over, making the sea very salty.

In the Extreme

When living things die, moisture in the air helps them **decay**. In the desert, the air is so dry that a dead body dries out and shrinks. It becomes **mummified**. Graves in the Takla Makan Desert of China have human mummies that are 3,800 years old.

7

DESERT PLANTS

Plants that live in the desert must be able to collect as much water as possible and then hang on to it—or die!

THE ROOT OF THE PROBLEM

When it does rain in the desert, it is often a very heavy downpour that does not last long. The water soaks into the sand quickly or travels along dry riverbeds. Plant roots have to be quick to collect the water.

SPREAD WIDE

The creosote bush has a huge network of shallow roots. That way it can soak up every drop of water in a big area around it. It can live for two years with no water at all.

▲ *Welwitschia plants grow slowly in the dry conditions, but they can live for a long time—some are more than 1,000 years old!*

GOING DEEP

Some desert plants have very deep roots called tap roots. A good example of this is the Welwitschia plant found in the Namib Desert. This plant has a fast-growing root that goes several feet into the ground. Above ground, the plant has only two large ragged leaves, which stop the plant from losing too much water through evaporation. When it does not rain, the Welwitschia collects water from fog.

LEAVES AND STEMS

Most desert plants do not have the same kind of leaves as plants in other regions. Water evaporates quickly from wide flat leaves. Instead, plants in deserts have narrow leaves or needles. Some, such as **cacti**, do not have any leaves at all. They are just one big stem.

▼ *Fig marigolds are called living stones. These tiny plants have only two leaves. They usually have the same shape and color of the stones around them to protect themselves from hungry animals.*

SAVING WATER

Succulent plants, such as aloes, store water in thick, wax-covered leaves. The wax stops water vapor escaping from inside the leaf. The flat, rounded pads of a prickly pear are not leaves but wide stems. The plant stores its water in its stem.

▼ *Aloe leaves are filled with sticky liquid.*

DESERT TREE

A Joshua tree is not a tree at all, but a yucca—a succulent plant— in the Mojave Desert in California. They grow very slowly. The tallest trees are 150 years old. The fibers from the Joshua tree's stem is used to weave baskets and shoes and to make paper.

PLANT PORES

Plants have **pores** in their leaves used to breathe gases in and out. Most plants open their pores during the day. However, desert plants keep them shut during the day and open them at night when it is cool. This prevents precious water from escaping through the pores.

Vital Statistics

★ Baobab trees (below) grow in dry parts of southern Africa and India. Some are 2,000 years old.

★ People dig into the trunks to reach stored water or build a shelter.

★ The trees' large fruits contain a sweet pulp, which is known as monkey bread.

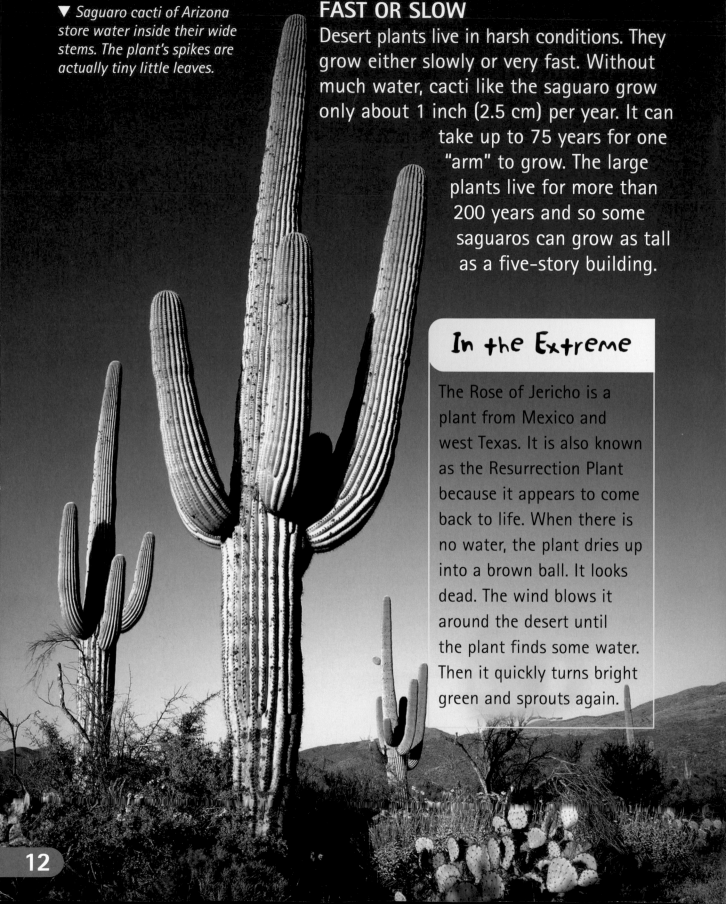

▼ *Saguaro cacti of Arizona store water inside their wide stems. The plant's spikes are actually tiny little leaves.*

FAST OR SLOW

Desert plants live in harsh conditions. They grow either slowly or very fast. Without much water, cacti like the saguaro grow only about 1 inch (2.5 cm) per year. It can take up to 75 years for one "arm" to grow. The large plants live for more than 200 years and so some saguaros can grow as tall as a five-story building.

In the Extreme

The Rose of Jericho is a plant from Mexico and west Texas. It is also known as the Resurrection Plant because it appears to come back to life. When there is no water, the plant dries up into a brown ball. It looks dead. The wind blows it around the desert until the plant finds some water. Then it quickly turns bright green and sprouts again.

BIG BLOOMERS

Desert sand is often full of **dormant** seeds. In parts of the Sonoran Desert there can be 1,000 seeds in every square foot of soil (10,000 per square m). When conditions are right, these seeds sprout, making the sands burst into color (*left*). The seeds are tough. Scientists have found 300–year-old seeds in mud bricks. They were still alive and bloomed into flowers!

TAKING TIME

Other desert plants are active for only short periods of time. They are called ephemerals. They include the desert paintbrush, rockroses, and verbena. Their seeds lie dormant for a long time. The seeds must sometimes wait years for the right conditions. Then they complete their life cycle very quickly before it gets too hot and all the water is gone. Some can grow, flower, and produce seeds in just three weeks. Plants in Namaqualand in Namibia and South Africa put on a brilliant display of color in the spring. Millions of flowers bloom in a matter of days.

▼ *The desert paintbrush grows across the North American West. Its red flowers are easy to see among the rocks and sand.*

DESERT ANIMALS

Animals in the desert have three problems. They must find water in the driest places on Earth. They also need to cope with the heat. Then they look for food—plants and other animals—in places where few living things survive.

WITHOUT WATER

Animals that live in deserts have to survive with very little water. Camels are the largest desert residents. They can survive without water for about 50 days, as long as there is some food to eat. Camels can survive without any food for weeks using fat stored in their humps.

FOG BEETLES

It rarely rains in the Namib Desert but cool sea breezes bring thick fog at dawn. Each morning, darkling beetles climb to the top of the huge dunes (*above*). Then they do a headstand! Droplets of fog **condense** on the beetles' backs and run down their bodies into their mouth. This is called fog basking.

Water-holding frogs live in puddles in Australia. When the water dries out, the frogs burrow into the mud. As the ground dries into hard soil, the frogs stay damp inside **cocoons** of dried skin. They can stay underground for months.

▲ *A sandgrouse can carry water in the feathers on its belly. It takes a supply of water back to the nest for its chicks.*

DESERT NEIGHBORS

There are two **species** of camels. Bactrian camels have two humps. They live in the deserts of Central Asia. Dromedaries have one hump. They live in Africa and the Middle East. Both types can close their nostrils tightly to keep sand out during **sandstorms**.

OUT OF THE HEAT

Animals living in the desert have to protect themselves from the heat. Many animals are **nocturnal**—they sleep during the day and are active at night when it is cooler. Other animals remain dormant until the rains come. During cold weather, we call this **hibernation**. However, in hot weather it is called **estivation**.

▼ *The caracal is an African relative of the lynx and bobcat. It has fur on the soles of its feet to stop them from burning on the hot sand.*

Grasshopper mice are meat-eaters that live in the deserts of North America. The mouse stalks prey, such as insects, and kills them with a single bite. The mouse also defends its territory by howling like a tiny wolf (*below*).

BIG EARS

The fennec fox stands only about eight inches (20 cm) tall at its shoulder. But its ears are enormous! They can be up to six inches (15 cm) long. The huge ears have a lot of blood vessels running through them. That makes the ears work like a car radiator—the hot blood is cooled down by the air, stopping the fox's body from getting too hot. The ears are also very sensitive and can hear insect prey scurrying across the sand in the dark.

◄ *The fennec fox of southern Africa is the smallest member of the dog family.*

TAKE A BREATHER

African lungfish live like other fish when there is plenty of water. When the water starts to dry up, they burrow into the mud and make a chamber to estivate in. Like other fish, the lungfish breathe with **gills** under water. However, when they are underground, the fish breathe air with lungs before wriggling out again when the rain returns (*right*).

AIR CONDITIONING

Termites live inside giant mounds made out of dried mud. Some termite mounds are 20 feet (six m) high. The desert sunshine makes it very hot inside a mound. The termites have an air-conditioning system to keep cool. Tunnels bring cold air up from deep under ground where it is always cool and damp. The cool air pushes the hot air out through a network of chimneys.

STAYING SAFE

Desert animals have many ways to protect themselves from **predators**. Some blend into their surroundings so they cannot be seen among the sand and rocks. The web-footed gecko is a little lizard from the Namib Desert. Its skin is see-through, which makes it almost impossible to spot. Other animals scare predators away. The desert horned lizard lives in the Sonoran and Mojave deserts. It is named after the spikes on its head. The lizard likes to bury itself in the sand, leaving only its eyes and mouth showing. When threatened, it will try to scratch with its horns. If that fails, the lizard squirts the attacker with blood from its eyes.

ROLL UP

The armadillo lizard of southern Africa has an unusual way of protecting itself. When it is threatened by a predator it rolls up into a ball with its tail in its mouth. The soft body parts are hidden inside the ball. The attacker can see only the heavily armored upper body.

In the Extreme

▼ The thorny devil of Australia has protective spikes on its body to make it painful to eat. The spikes also collect dew which flows through channels to the lizard's mouth.

The Gila monster of the Sonoran Desert is one of only two lizards to use **venom**. It does not inject it like a snake. Instead, it pours its poison into the wounds of its prey as it chews on them.

WATCHING OUT

Meerkats often stand upright. This is the way they warm themselves in the morning sun of the Kalahari Desert. It also helps them spot enemies in the distance so they can run to their burrows quickly.

▼ *Sandfish are lizards that look for insects and seeds on and under the sands of the Sahara and Arabian deserts.*

SAND SWIMMER

It is not easy to walk across sand. Web-footed geckos have flaps of skin between their toes. The wide feet push against the loose grains. The sandfish has wide scales on its flat toes that help it grip the sand. It uses its long tail and flexible, rounded body to slither across the sand. If the sandfish is under attack, it burrows down and "swims" through the sand.

Vital Statistics

★ The Jerboa is a small mouse. It is often called the desert rat.

★ It hops across the desert like a kangaroo and can leap up to three feet (one m) to escape its predators.

SIDEWAYS MOVES

The sidewinder is a desert snake. It is named for the way it moves. It throws its head forward first, followed by its body and finally its tail. Not only can it move quickly over loose sand this way, the snake also only has a small part of its body touching the hot sand at any one time.

PEOPLE AND DESERTS

Spending your days surrounded by desert is tough. However, people have found many ways to make a living in the world's deserts since the dawn of history.

FOOD AND WATER

Most desert people are **nomads**. They do not live in one place all year, but move from place to place so their animals can find food and water. Desert dwellers are good hunters and they gather food from the wild. Nothing is wasted—even animal **dung** is used for fuel.

USING NATURE

The San people live in the Kalahari Desert. They hunt with poison arrows. The poison is made from beetle grubs. They also use ostrich egg shells as water bottles.

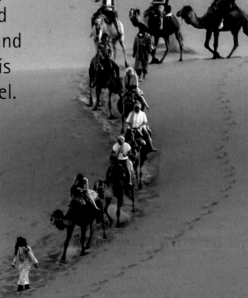

▼ Desert people travel in groups for safety. Traditionally, they form a caravan—the name for a convoy of camels.

◀ *The Dogon people live on the edge of the Sahara in Mali. They build grain stores made of stones and mud with thatched roofs. They protect the Dogon's food from mice.*

FAST FACTS

★ An oasis is a place where springs form pools in the desert.

★ People use oases as resting places when traveling across the desert.

★ Date Palms grow at an oasis, providing an important food source.

TOASTED INSECTS

The Aboriginal people living in the Australian Desert eat witchetty grubs. These large white caterpillars live inside shrub branches. The Aboriginal people say that when they are toasted on a fire the insects taste like scrambled eggs.

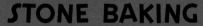

STONE BAKING

The Bedouin people of the Middle East cook food in the desert using stones. They dig a pit in the ground lined with flat rocks. A fire is built inside to heat the stones and when there is nothing but ashes, food, such as flat bread (*left*), is placed on the hot stones to cook.

MAKING SHELTER

Different desert **civilizations** have found ways to stay out of the heat. Some carry tents or build temporary shelters out of mud or branches. Others make use of shady cliffs or caves to escape the desert heat.

ROCK HOMES

Native American people lived in the deserts of southwestern United States about 1,000 years ago. They built their homes on ledges in canyons and cliffs. In many places, the only way to reach these villages was by ropes or rock climbing.

In the Extreme

Australians call their desert the Outback. The Outback mining town of Coober Pedy can reach 131 °F (55 °C) some days. People have built houses underground (*below*), where it is always much cooler. Some of the underground homes have swimming pools. There is even a church down there!

FAST FACTS

★ Bedouins live in black tents. They are divided by curtains—one side is for men, the other is for women.

★ Mongolian nomads in the Gobi Desert live in tents made from **felt**. This thick material keeps the family warm on cold desert nights.

Vital Statistics

★ Adobe is a type
of mud house built
in the southwestern
United States.

★ Straw is added
to help make the
bricks stronger.

★ Villages made
from adobe houses
are called *pueblos*.

▼ The Cliff Palace is a ruined
village in Colorado. About 800
years ago, 150 people lived there.

25

▶ *As well as making cotton clothes, Hopi men weave colorful baskets from desert plants, such as yuccas.*

▲ *Deserts are good places to find ancient carvings or paintings on rock walls. The images do not fade away in the dry conditions.*

SURVIVAL SKILLS

Living in the desert is hard work. Many hours each day are taken up finding food and water and building shelters. Everyone has to help: in different civilizations men and women do certain jobs. In most civilizations, it is the women who make baskets and clothes. However, this is a man's job among the Hopi people of Arizona.

COUNTDOWN

Without water or shelter from the heat, you could survive only two or three days in a desert. **Dehydration** is the biggest danger. Your body needs water for sweat to keep itself cool. As you run out of water, your blood thickens into goo, your eyes dry out, and you go blind. Your brain gets too hot to work, and you pass out and die.

When a Hopi couple gets married, the groom weaves all the wedding outfits.

PASSING ON

The Bedouin mark their graves with a stone at the head and one at the feet. They traditionally leave the clothes of the dead person on top of the grave for any poor people passing by who might need them.

THE BLUE MEN

The Tuareg of the Sahara are known as the "Blue Men." They are famous for headgear colored with indigo. A Tuareg man is given his veil at the age of 18 years old. The veil helps protect his face during sandstorms.

Vital Statistics

★ The didgeridoo is a wind instrument used by the Aboriginal people of Australia.

★ The instrument (*left*) is made from a branch hollowed out by termites.

★ Didgeridoo music is an important part of Aboriginal ceremonies.

EXTREME FACTS

DESERT ANTELOPE

The addax antelope (*right*) is one of the rarest animals in the world. It lives in the Sahara Desert. Desert people hunted the addax for its meat and skin. There are now only 250 of them living in the wild. There are about 3,000 more living in zoos and wildlife parks around the world.

EXTREME RACING

Every year, athletes gather in Morocco for the Marathon des Sables—the Marathon of the Sands. The race is run through the desert (*left*) over six days. Competitors run a total of six marathons in that time. The race organizers supply the racers with water and put up tents each night. However, the competitors must carry all their food and clothing with them in a rucksack when running. Lahcen Ahansal of Morocco has won the race 10 times!

LAB WORK

You can make your own quicksand using cornstarch. You will need a 16-ounce (450-g) box of cornstarch, one or two cups of water, a large plastic mixing bowl, and a spoon. Put one quarter of the cornstarch in the bowl and stir in half a cup of water. Mix them together—using your hands is easiest. Slowly add the rest of the starch and water until the mixture is thick but runny like honey. Now, try to push your hand fast into the mixture. It will feel solid. Next lower your hand into the bowl slowly. Watch your hand gently sink!

SOFT GROUND

Deserts have areas of quicksand, where sand is mixed with water. It looks solid but you sink into it and get stuck. One of the largest areas of quicksand is the Dasht-e Kavir in Iran (*above*).

TEMPERATURE RECORD

The hottest day ever recorded was 136° F (58 °C) in the Sahara Desert in 1922.

RED ROCK

Uluru, once named Ayres Rock (*below*), in the Australian desert is the largest single piece of rock in the world. It is 1,100 feet (335 m) high.

GLOSSARY

basin Low area surrounded by mountains

cacti Plants with spikes instead of leaves

civilizations Organized societies

cocoons Protective cases

condense To turn from a gas into a liquid

continent A large area of land; there are seven continents: Asia, Africa, Australia, Europe, North America, South America, and Antarctica

decay To break apart naturally

dehydration To run out of water

dormant In a sleep-like state

drought A time when no rain falls and the land becomes very dry

dung Animal droppings

estivation Being dormant to avoid the heat of the summer

evaporates When water turns into gas when it is heated

felt Material made from animal hairs

gills Body parts used by fish and other animals to breathe in water

gold rush A period when a lot of people travel to an area to dig for gold

hibernation Being dormant to avoid the cold of winter

minerals Naturally occurring chemicals

mummified To be preserved from decay

NASA The U.S. space agency

nocturnal To come out at night

nomads People who travel from place to place instead of living at one location

pores Tiny holes

predator Hunting animal

sandstorms High winds that blow clouds of sand around the desert

species A group of closely related animals or plants

succulent A plant with thick leaves

tropics The warm region of Earth on either side of the equator

vapor A gas, such as water vapor

venom A poison used by animals to kill prey or enemies

FURTHER RESOURCES

BOOKS

101 Facts About Deserts by Julia Barnes. Milwaukee, WI: Gareth Stevens Publishing, 2004.

Deserts: Thirsty Wonderlands by Laura Purdie Salas. Minneapolis, MN: Picture Window Books, 2007.

I Live in the Desert by Gini Holland. Milwaukee, WI: Weekly Reader Early Learning Library, 2004.

Survivor's Science in the Desert by Peter D. Riley. Chicago, IL: Raintree, 2005.

The Dry Desert: A Web of Life by Philip Johansson. Berkeley Heights, NJ: Enslow Publishers, 2004.

WEBSITES

Camel Facts

fohn.net/camel-pictures-facts/index.html

Namib Desert dunes

science.nationalgeographic.com/science/enlarge/ namib-desert-dunes.html

National Geographic video about the deserts of China

video.nationalgeographic.com/video/player/places/ parks-and-nature-places/cave-canyon-desert/china_desert.html

INDEX

Printed in the U.S.A. — BG